Nothing Left Unsaid

Nothing Left Unsaid

Words to Help You
and Your Loved Ones through
the Hardest Times

Carol Orsborn

CONARI PRESS
Berkeley, California

Conari Press books are distributed by Publishers Group West.

ISBN: 1-57324-565-8

Cover Photography: Courtesy of Photonica.
Sunflower, Front and Back by Jun Kishimoto
Cover and Book Design: Suzanne Albertson

LIBRARY OF CONGRESS CATALOGING-IN-PUBLICATION DATA

Orsborn, Carol.
Nothing left unsaid : words to help you and your loved ones
through the hardest times / Carol Orsborn.
p.   cm.
Includes bibliographical references.
ISBN 1-57324-565-8
1. Sick—Religious life.   2. Terminally ill—Religious life.   I. Title.
BL625.9.S53 O77 2001
291.4'42–dc21
00–012573

Printed in Canada on recycled paper.

01 02 03 04   TR   10 9 8 7 6 5 4 3 2 1

for
Dad

Nothing Left Unsaid

PART II

Rituals for Healing and Resolution

PART III

Questions for Conversation
or Journaling

Introduction

Tending Love's Flame

Words are powerful. When spoken from our hearts, our words have the capacity to grow love and minimize regret. Words can heal old wounds, ease transitions, and give hope.

Perhaps as you hold these pages in your hands, you are realizing the preciousness of time, hoping to find the right words to speak while there is still the opportunity to express your deepest feelings to someone for whom you care. It is possible, too, that you are hoping to bring a sense of resolution to memories from the past by speaking words left unsaid between a parent and a child, husband and wife, or a friend or relative from long ago.

However you have arrived at this moment, it may well feel that life has given you an impossible task, asking more of you than you have to give. The sages teach us, however, that the depth of pain you are feeling is a direct reflection of the degree of love you have allowed into your life. Pain, like love, has no boundaries. If you did not love so much, you would not feel so much. This is the price that those who love deeply are bound to pay. The amount of pain you feel is not a sign of your inadequacy—rather, it is an acknowledgment of your capacity to love fully.

1

In the months before I sat down to write this book, I, too, was living through a time when everything mattered and each word was important. My father lay in the hospital, critically ill, family members sitting vigil beside him for many long weeks. Sometimes, our words flowed and an indescribable peace descended upon us. Other times, we struggled to find something to say or hear that would help us get it right. We didn't always succeed.

At one critical point, overwhelmed and exhausted, I gave myself reluctant permission to wander into the too-bright light of day outside the hospital's walls and into a bookstore across the street. I found reassurance in the familiar surroundings and the promise of wise words that could help me make it through the day. Understanding the seriousness of the situation while continuing to hold hope for the future, I longed not only for guidance through the emotional complexities of my extended family's relationships, but to find ways to get in touch with what it was I really wanted to say to and hear from my father while there was still time. Perhaps there would be a book I could read aloud to my father and family that would give words to the feelings and thoughts we all struggled to express.

Just spending a few moments in the bookstore was comforting to me—even though I didn't find the book I was searching for during my brief foray there. When I could no longer bear to stay away, I returned to my father's room. I was fortunate. Despite the seriousness of the prognosis, including a week in a coma and an extended period of rehabilitation, my dad miraculously recovered. I am grateful for this gift of time my dad and I have received. We are using this time well, experiencing the bittersweet joy of knowing that nothing has been left unsaid.

There have been other searches in my life, some more satisfying than others, for just the right words. I have let friends' and family's letters, phone calls, and e-mails go unanswered and then longed to find the courage to say the words that would help us reconnect, sometimes too late. I have lost a child to miscarriage, still yearning years later, hoping for a sense of completion, to find the words I never had the chance to share. I have shared my husband's search for his birth father, hoping that the words he practiced over and over again would somehow be answered, only to find that his father had already passed away. And finally, I have tasted my own mortality, trying to get it right with my children and husband in those tender and raw days after my own diagnoses of breast cancer four years ago, when it was I, not my father, who lay in a hospital bed searching for words of comfort for my family.

We who have answered life's cry take up the sacred task of tending love's flame through the dark night. We dig deep to find the words we've previously neglected to say, feel things we've never realized were there before, all the while confronting a humbling reality that in many ways, faced with the mystery of the infinite, we know less than ever before. Even as we cling to the last remnants of the way things should or used to be, destiny pushes us off the

A Word about This Book

I wrote this book out of my life experiences and theological studies to provide comfort and resolution for you and those you love. It is my hope that this book be a support to you, whatever the nature of the challenges you are facing.

You may prefer to read this book privately, or you may want to share it aloud with others. As you read, pause from time to time to reflect on how these words connect to your life. Notice the particular words or thoughts that catch your attention. Without trying, you will find your heart opening to a comforting presence, speaking to you through the pages of this book. Allow that presence to empower these words to speak directly and personally to you and to those for whom you care.

Following this introductory material, the book consists of three parts. Part I contains readings, stories, prayers, and affirmations drawn from a broad spectrum of religious and spiritual traditions. Part II consists of rituals and processes that will help you and the one for whom you care find resolution, healing, and peace. In part III there are questions for you to consider. You can respond to these silently, writing your answers down in a journal, or use the questions as the basis of meaningful conversation with your loved ones.

May this book help you to grow your love and minimize your regret, come what may. And may you come to use the power of words and spirit to transform whatever you are facing in your life into sacred space.

PART I

Stories, Poems,
and Prayers
for
Reading Silently
or Aloud

CHAPTER 1

A Strange New Land

When You Can't Find Words for What You Feel

THE CRYING BUDDHA

There came a time when a rabbi was invited to visit a synagogue of great repute, some distance away. The rabbi and his disciples traveled many days and nights, anticipating their arrival at the synagogue.

When at last the rabbi and his disciples reached the synagogue, he hesitated at the door, refusing to enter. His disciples asked him what was wrong.

"I sense only joy and praise," the rabbi explained.

"What could be wrong with this?" asked the disciples, for this seemed to them to provide the greatest encouragement to go inside.

When they pressed the question, the rabbi explained, "Words spoken without honesty and humility cannot rise to heaven. The people here want only to show off how good they look to God. We must travel on until we find a place where the people are aware of their inadequacy."

9

The sacred space where life summons us to attend someone for whom we care is such a place. There are times in our lives when our hearts are filled with sorrow, not celebration. There are times when we feel anxiety, doubt, and fear instead of certainty.

When I was first summoned to my ailing father's side, overwhelmed by love and pain, I struggled to find the words big enough to contain my feelings. I wanted to say just the right things to my father. And I wanted to find meaning and resolution in his responses. Sometimes I succeeded at this, sometimes I did not.

Had it not been for the gift of a crying Buddha some years before, I would have been tempted to judge myself for my inadequacies. Instead, I remembered the lessons I had learned about the true nature of competence and compassion nearly ten years ago as a result of a good friend's gift to me.

To tell the truth, when the crying Buddha first made his entrance into my life, I did not welcome him. The event was a going-away party for my family, gathering our friends around us one last time to say good-bye. The journey we were to make was self-chosen: the move from the familiar comfort of our long-time home in San Francisco to the unknown challenges of a new life in Nashville. It was hard saying good-bye. And perhaps to dull the pain, I spent more time thinking and talking giddily about the adventure to come than I did about the loss that was inevitable.

And then one of my closest friends gave me a small wrapped package. I anticipated perfume or perhaps a heart-shaped necklace. I remember that I was laughing as I tore away the tissue, carrying on a lighthearted conversation with one friend while another was clipping ribbons from the gifts into my hair. Even when the small dark object was mostly exposed, I could not guess what it was. Perhaps it was a pretty wooden ball, or a paperweight. And then I took it into my hands and recognized the meaning. Carved into the wood was a heavy head bent down, weeping into its arms.

I disliked that little Buddha. It reminded me that with this transition would come pain and loss. The last thing I wanted to deal with was the fact that even if my friend and I kept our pledges to stay in touch, something was ending. My friend saw the stricken look on my face.

"Maybe you'll never need this little guy," she said, hugging me close. "But it's a good thing to have around in case of emergencies."

I thought about leaving the Buddha behind, preferring the gifts of perfume and roses. But somehow he got packed and forgotten. It wasn't until weeks later, in tears while unpacking one last box of knick-knacks, that I stumbled across the sad little Buddha. Suddenly, I realized that my friend had been telling me that I was beloved—embraced by compassion—no matter how frightened or lonely I might at some point be. She was letting me know that the fully lived life is not about being any one way:

happy or angry or whatever. It's about being real. When you are sad, you're really sad. When you're joyful, you're really joyful.

The little unwrapped Buddha reminded me of a story I had once heard of two spiritual disciples who meet at the bank of a river. The first cannot help bragging about his guru.

"My teacher is so fantastic. You won't believe the miracles he can do. Why, he can stand on the bank of the river with a paintbrush in his hand and his self-portrait gets painted on the other side. He can levitate. He can materialize gold out of thin air. What can your guru do?"

"Simply this," the second disciple responds. "When he's hungry, he eats. When he's tired, he sleeps."

Immediately, the first disciple bowed to the second and became enlightened.

Remembering the crying Buddha, I realized that I had found the key to trusting that the words I searched for would be there when I needed them, and if they weren't there, that too would be all right. The secret is this: Before you start worrying about what to say or how to interpret what you hear, you need to give yourself permission to tell the whole truth about how you're feeling, what you're thinking, to yourself. Without censoring, judging, or suppressing your doubt, anger, resentment, fear, or despair, trust yourself to be whatever it is you truly are in that moment. You don't need to do anything about what you are feeling. Sometimes it takes courage and wisdom to be patient with yourself, allowing truth and clarity to emerge from the mists of confusion and resistance in their own time and way. Be gentle with yourself, and when the moment is right, the words you most need to speak or hear will come as a by-product of your honest response to life's summons.

The crying Buddha teaches us that the secret to living a full life is to become willing to embrace whatever comes our way. To be fully alive is to stand and embrace the broader range of human experience: bittersweet sadness, righteous anger, compassionate concern, even deep and honest despair. You must be willing to surrender the illusion that this is your show, and allow your heart to break open. It is through these cracks that healing enters and stirs your heart and soul to their fullest expression.

The crying Buddha teaches us that there is divinity in everything—even the painful parts. If you are happy, that is laughing Buddha. If you are sad, that is crying Buddha. The crying Buddha teaches us that to fulfill your true human potential you must first be fully alive.

∾ Into the Forest

You have journeyed to the forest many times,
   admiring the landscape.
You have taken refuge in the leafy shadow of the oak,
   the newly sprouted pine.
And did you remember, too, to celebrate
   the broken tree limbs and
      blackened stumps stricken by lightning?
The loving soul's journey has taken us over and over
again
   into the woods.
At last, we understand that bare stumps and empty space
   are not imperfections in the forest,
      but the forest, itself.
Can you find it in your heart to embrace it all?

∾ No Need to Know

Let sadness flow freely where it will
>like a river grateful for its banks
>clearing away outgrown beliefs
>soothing jagged edges
>splintering logjams
>not needing to know where the journey ends
>content to forge a deeper channel
>>for the joy to come.

❧ Fulfill Your True Human Potential

Love can grow so large it breaks your heart.
Compassion for another can set your soul on fire.
Clarity of vision can shatter your everyday illusions.
Life can leave you shivering naked and awestruck
    before the mystery.

Who says the spiritual path leads only to happiness?

CHAPTER 2

The Language of Love

*When There Is Something You'd Really
Like to Say or Hear*

TELLING STORIES

When my dad was in the hospital, seriously ill, there was something simple about my love for him. I knew what I wanted from him: I wanted him to get better and let life go on the way it had been before he got sick. I wanted him to tell me what a good daughter I have been: that the good outweighed the bad and that all is forgiven. I wanted him to admit to his shortcomings too and to assure me that they were not meant to sting. I wanted to hear him sing his songs again. In fact, I didn't want to miss a thing. Suddenly, I was full of questions about his parents, his childhood, his training as a physician during hard times. When he was alert, I begged him to tell me again how he eloped with Mother. Remind me of the words to the poem he wrote for Harrison High and the story he used to tell me when I was a child about the lions and the chrysanthemums.

Dad loves to tell stories almost as much as he loves to sing. They are often the same stories, told so often they have become family ritual.

17

After some time in the hospital had already slowly passed, the physician decided there was no option other than to operate on Dad. I did not expect a story from Dad. Neither did I think he had any new stories to tell. But I was surprised on both counts.

Despite his discomfort and the effort it obviously took, Dad wanted to share a story with me about something that had happened to him during World War II. Stationed in the Philippines, far away from home, he had bonded deeply with his companions. Medics, sent to care for those injured and ailing on the front lines, he and his companions lived through dangerous times together.

Then, for no apparent reason, there was a lull in the fighting. Shortly after, a dispatch arrived, offering the medics much-needed R&R. The boys were free to take the day and go to swim in a lake nearby. Dad readied himself for the celebration, but soon a second dispatch arrived. This one contained orders that Dad, only, was to be shifted later that afternoon from his companions to a new battalion many miles away. He would have to say good-bye to his friends while he waited for the transport to arrive that would take him to his new assignment.

His friends hugged Dad an emotional farewell, then boarded the company's Jeep. Dad stood there a good long time, listening to their laughter and singing fade into silence, feeling alone and abandoned.

Every moment he waited for his transport to come felt like an eternity. And of course, the transport was hours late. When the driver finally arrived, he apologized, explaining that there had been an accident and the road had been closed. "A Jeep, carrying a group of medics, careened off the road and over the side of the cliff into the lake below. All were instantly killed."

Dad paused to take a deep breath, then went on to finish his story quietly.

"I would have been on that Jeep, having nothing more serious on my mind than going swimming with my buddies at the lake."

I know what Dad was saying to me. He did not explicitly use the words "Life is precious," or "Every day has been a gift." But these words, and more, were in the squeeze of his hand before he drifted off into sleep.

As I stood there beside him, thinking about his story, my mind wandered back to the sunny afternoon more than forty years ago when Dad had run beside my wobbly two-wheeler, teaching me to ride. As long as his hand made contact with my arm, the bike stayed upright and I felt like I was riding on my own. But the moment he withdrew his hand, the bike would suddenly careen and crash. Eventually, of course, I pedaled faster than even he could run. Until this moment, I had not remembered the last time I felt his hand on my shoulder; I had only remembered the first time I took off down the road holding strong and steady.

I had taken so much for granted in my life. Suddenly, I was overwhelmed with gratitude for it all. There were no words that could communicate my feelings, so we just kept on telling stories and sharing memories—until the very last moment they came to get Dad and roll him away to surgery.

The stories and memories we shared were simple and sweet. And yet, just being together—sometimes speaking our thoughts, sometimes sitting in silence—some kind of completion was taking place that went far beyond the words that were being spoken.

Perhaps this is something of what Ivan Pavlov, the father of behavioral psychology, experienced while he lay in bed, consumed by fever. Before the discovery of antibiotics, few held hope for his recovery from a life-threatening infection. Seemingly delirious, he instructed his assistant to go down to the river near his home and return with a bucket of sun-warmed mud. Humoring Pavlov, the aid duly brought the bucket of mud to his bed. Shaky and weak, the great psychologist dipped his hands into the bucket and started to play with the oozy brown clay. Within a few hours, Pavlov's fever had broken.

After his recovery, Pavlov was asked to explain his odd behavior. He answered with a story about his childhood. He explained that when he was young, he had often gone down to the river with his mother. While she did the laundry, he enjoyed playing near her with the clay of the riverbank. As he played in the mud, she would tell him wonderful stories.

The mud he had asked to be brought to his bed represented the time in his life when he felt most peaceful. As he lay ill in bed, he reasoned that if he could recreate this favorite time in his life, he would give his body the best chance to recover. His healing began the exact moment he thought to request the mud.

On the good days, Dad's stories and my memories wove together in a tapestry of love that was palpable. Regardless of the prognosis, there was something deeply healing about what we shared. When I was with him, time slowed down. A cup of coffee became a sacrament. Flowers sent by family friends recreated Eden. The nurse's gentle humor was the funniest thing I'd ever heard. Even the orderly who emptied the bags of fluid did so within our sacred space. Without trying, the stories and memories we shared carried with them healing, love, and resolution.

∾

Here is a lesson from the rabbinic tradition that illustrates the power of a heartfelt story.

It is told that when Rabbi Israel Shem Tov saw misfortune threatening his people, he went to a special place in the forest to meditate. He would light a fire, say a certain prayer, and intercede with God.

When his disciple, the Maggid of Mezritch, was faced with the same task for his generation, he would go to the same place and say, "Master of the Universe, Listen! I do not know how to light the fire, but I am still able to say the prayer."

Still later, Rabbi Moshe-leib of Sasov went to the forest to help his people, saying, "I do not know how to light the fire. I do not know the prayer, but I know the place and that must be sufficient."

Then it was up to Rabbi Israel of Rizhin to appeal to God. Sitting in his chair, his head in his hands, he said, "I am unable to light the fire. I do not know the prayer. I cannot even find the place in the forest. All I can do is tell the story."

Sometimes, all any of us can do is tell the story. It is enough.

∾ One Heart

I sit here,

    immersed in thoughts and feelings about you.

Time stops and the world recedes.

This is sacred space,

    where everyday matters cannot penetrate.

Time stretches out and embraces us.

Now that I have realized we share the same heart,

    I know I'll never be the same again.

And it's all right.

∾ Our Moment

That so many have been here before
　　gives perspective and some small comfort
　　but does not come close to touching the truth
　　　　that this is our moment:
　　　　exquisite and unique.

It is our turn to be the center of the universe,
　　to indulge ourselves at the banquet of emotions
　　to drink deeply of every feeling as if for the first time
　　and then to breathe together quietly, our hearts full.

∾ *Recognizing Love*

Our souls know love.
> they recognize their own.

Sometimes it's a flash of recognition,
> like a silvery fish rising above the surface of the pond
> before descending again into the eddies and flows of
>> daily life.

Other times it's a slow, old turtle steadily making its way
> through the mud at the bottom.

Search the depths to think of a time you recognized the
> truth of love,
And you will find home.

CHAPTER 3

Time to Heal

When You Really Want to Get It Right

THE FISHERMEN'S PRAYER

Some things you really want to get right. When my father was being taken away for his serious operation, I didn't think it was asking too much of life to be able to say or hear two or three meaningful words, like "I love you," "Forgive me," or "Good-bye" one more time.

Say these words a thousand times, and you can still come up just two or three syllables shy. We worry about the possibility that we may not say or hear everything we long for. Or that we may realize what we want to share, ask, or hear—but it will be too late.

I remember some time ago when I was studying for my brown belt in karate. My wise sensei saw how hard I was working, and how fearful I was of the test to come. He took me aside.

"Understand something," he said to me. "You won't pass because of something you do special or different on the one day of the exam. You will pass because of all the years of practice you have already invested. Your everyday self is all that is necessary."

27

The same is true of important moments in our relationships. I thought that having had breast cancer, accepting the inevitability of mortality, I had accepted my imperfection. But now, faced with this new challenge of my father's illness, I began to realize that even if I admitted that this was not my show, I had tried at the very least to keep control of the script. I had monitored each word that passed between me and my father, searching for hidden meanings. I had treasured some, rejected others. But when you surrender yourself to life, you don't get to pick and choose the pieces you'll keep and the ones you'll release. Like my karate sensei taught me, the truth of who and what you and your relationships are is not about what you do or say on any one occasion, but is the sum total of how you choose to live your life every day.

In the Christian tradition, the story is told of three fishermen who have something to teach us how to live our lives every day. A bishop's ship is scheduled to pay a rare visit to a remote island. As the bishop disembarks to stroll along the sandy seashore, he comes across three fishermen mending their nets. In broken English, the fishermen explained that centuries before, this island had been visited by a missionary. They proudly tell the bishop that their ancestors had become Christians. Impressed, the bishop asks them to recite the Lord's Prayer. Dutifully, the three fishermen turn their gaze upward and recite in unison, "We are three, you are three, have mercy on us."

Appalled at the primitive prayer, the bishop spent the day teaching them the correct words to the Lord's Prayer. The fishermen tried as hard as they could, at last giving the bishop the satisfaction of hearing the prayer said correctly. Months later, the bishop's ship returned to the area of the fishermen's island. The bishop looked up and noticed a light approaching the ship from the east. Astonished, the bishop recognized the three fishermen walking on top of the sea toward his boat.

"Bishop," they cried out when at last they were close enough to be heard. "We have an important question to ask you. We are so very, very sorry but we forgot the words to your prayer. We start out fine but then we forget. Please teach us the words again."

The bishop was silent for a moment, then he replied, "Go back to your island, my brothers, and each time you pray, say, 'We are three, you are three, have mercy on us.'"

When you exhaust yourself worrying about getting things the way you think they are supposed to be, you sink. Only when you become willing to embrace the wider range of human possibilities do you become connected to the whole. This, then, is sacred space: the realm of the true mystic. This is not tamed order, delivering you the words you want in reward for your good behavior. Rather, this is the wild space where life sends you deep into the mystery of love and faith.

∾ *The Quest for Perfection*

We hope to take full advantage of every opportunity to
   support healing:
      to understand everything that has eluded us,
      to resolve all our life's issues,
      to mend our relationships and mature spiritually.

But our aspirations, even as lofty as these,
   exhaust us and keep us busy striving
   at a time when we need to make space for quiet and
      peace.

It will be healing enough when you can lay aside your
         self-assessments and demands,
   and stop trying so hard to get this right.

Indulge, instead, in being an ordinary person who loves
   God.

~ *Feeling Lost*

Sacred space has no map.
Sacred time no clock.

If you feel lost,
>   it is only because you think
>   there is someplace else you should be.

Throw away
>   the instruction books,
>   the directions,
>   the guides.

You are the only one who has ever lived
>   this moment of your life.
Why not trust that you are already doing exactly what
  you should
And that it is enough?

∾ *There Isn't Enough Time*

At times, we struggle with the fear that there isn't
enough time.
Of course, there are things we'd still like to change,
    good to be done,
    words yet to say.
But we ask only for time enough to fulfill God's purpose
for us
    and to live our whole lives.

In sacred time, you can stop racing the clock,
    wasting your precious energy
    and become a witness to God's inviolable promise:

In God's eyes,
living our whole lives is something we all do.

∾ Exhausting Yourself

If thoughts of recovery, cures, and miracles consume you,
   what of you will be left to heal?

Busy yourself instead with love,
      and you create the environment in which
         healing will most readily take place.

CHAPTER 4

Hills and Valleys

When It's Time to Say the Hard Things

THE WISDOM OF INTEGRITY

Sometimes it feels as if the spiritual journey leads us not toward the light, but into darkness. We can feel overwhelmed by our shortcomings and by our resentment of others. There are things we know we could or should say to help make things right. And, too, not taking the risk of asking another for what one needs to hear—is that not also a shortcoming crying out for rectification? Where does one begin?

The answer is this: The moment you discontinue making choices that cause suffering to you or to others is the very moment recovery begins. You restore your integrity when you expose the broken places in your spirit, feeling whatever emotions arise. You heed your intention to set things right, and whenever possible, you act on your intentions. Of course you hope for certain responses and results. You want to be forgiven, you want to hear that you are loved. But understand that it is in your willingness to feel the pain and in your sincere intention that accompanies the restoration of integrity—

35

and not necessarily in the results—that true healing begins.

I am reminded here of a story told by Pema Chödrön, director of Gampo Abbey, the first Tibetan monastery in North America established for Westerners. It is the story of Milarepa, one of the lineage holders of Kagyü Tibetan Buddhism.

> Milarepa was a hermit, passing many years alone trying to achieve perfect peace by meditating in the caves of Tibet. One night he returned to his cave after gathering firewood only to discover that demons had taken over his abode. There was a demon reading Milarepa's book; there was one sleeping in his bed. They were all over the place. Hoping to control the situation, Milarepa came up with an idea. He would teach them about spirituality. He found a seat higher than theirs and began to lecture about compassion. The demons simply ignored him. Then he got angry and charged at them. They simply laughed at him. Finally he gave up, sitting down on the floor of the cave with them, surrendering to the fact that since they would not be going away, they might as well learn to live together.

> At that moment, they left—all except one. Recognizing the need for total surrender, Milarepa had but one last resort. He walked over and put himself right into the mouth of the demon. He literally fed himself to his

demon. At that moment, the demon departed, leaving Milarepa alone but transformed.

Sometimes, the only way to make things right again is to feed yourself to that which you most fear. If there is something you yearn to hear somebody say to you, ask them for what you need now.

If you have wronged someone and can confess directly to the person you wounded, do it now. If you don't know what to say, say this: "Here is my authentic self, flaws and all. While I prefer that you love and forgive me, I am willing to accept the consequences."

If you are still not able to say what needs to be said aloud, turn to someone you trust and ask for help. Here are words to help you begin: "There is something that I regret that I cannot bring myself to say. I need help."

What gives us the courage to be vulnerable in this way? In their book about the Sufi poet Rumi, *Love, Soul and Freedom,* Denise Breton and Christopher Largent use their own as well as the poet's words to help explain that the call to return to wholeness "may lead us into a night . . . but at the same time, knowing that we're on the quest for our souls is what joy is. Grieving for our souls spares us the greater grief of forgetting our souls."

When we are faced with the hard stuff, we can offer the same generosity of spirit to ourselves that a character in Lorraine Hansberry's play *A Raisin in the Sun* extends to a wayward child:

There's always something left to love. And if you ain't learned that, you ain't learned nothing. Have you cried for that boy today? . . . What he been through and what it done to him. Child, when do you think is the time to love somebody the most; when they done good and made things easy for everybody? Well then, you ain't through learning—because that ain't the time at all. It's when he's at his lowest and can't believe in hisself 'cause the world done whipped him so. When you starts measuring somebody, measure him right, child, measure him right. Make sure you done taken into account what hills and valleys he come through before he got to wherever he is.

⌦ Judgment

Rabbi Elinelech Lizensker said,

"I am sure of my share in the World-to-Come.

When I stand to plead before the bar of the Heavenly
Tribunal,

    I will be asked,

'Did you learn, as is duty bound?'

To this, I will make answer: 'No.'

Again, I will be asked,

'Did you pray, as is duty bound?'

Again, my answer will be, 'No.'

The third question will be,

'Did you do good, as is duty bound?'

And for the third time, I will answer, 'No.'

Then judgment will be awarded in my favor,

    for I will have spoken the truth."

~ *If Only*

If only there were more time, some say,
    heading a long list of regrets.
If only there could be more healing,
    more rectification,
    more love.
As if what could happen in the future
    or didn't happen in the past
    is more powerful than what is happening right now.

What can we do about the past?
Where is the past now?
And what about the future?
How can we do anything about that
    which doesn't yet exist?
If all you have is right now,
    why waste precious moments feeling regret?

If you've got something to say, say it now!
If you want more rectification, rectify now!
If you want more love, love now!

∽ Out of Control

There was a time when you thought
    you were calling the shots in your life:
        Work hard,
        Be good,
        Be smart,
        Eat plenty of vegetables
        and things would turn out for you.

There was a time when you thought you knew things,
    when you protected your vulnerable places.
You felt big and strong and capable.

But in sacred space, things spin out of control.
Our tender places now stand exposed.

But in the emptiness that we once filled mostly with
ourselves
    there is now, at last, a hole large enough for God.

As You Are

We play the roles life give us:

    dances of anger, affection, disappointment, and joy. . .

    a wild ballet with many acts.

We laugh, we cry, we yell, we make up.

Beneath it all,

    the wry, sly awareness that we are putting on

    quite a show.

If I were to write the review, I'd say,

    "Don't change a thing."

And as for your performance:

    "I love you just the way you are."

CHAPTER 5

The Bottom of the Ocean

When Deeper Questions Beg for Attention

STIRRING HARD

The good friend who gave me the crying Buddha as a going-away present once suggested to me that our inner lives are like bowls of vegetable soup: If left to sit, all the goodies tend to sink to the bottom.

When circumstances shake up the ordinary patterns of our everyday lives, it is natural to find ourselves suddenly digging deep to ask bigger questions of life. Who are we, and what is life all about? Have I lived my life meaningfully, and have I fulfilled the purpose intended for me? Have I done all I could?

I remember that when my friend compared our lives to bowls of soup, she added that just about everybody has a most and least favorite vegetable. "What if you love carrots but hate onions?" she had said to me. "The flavor of the soup is made up of all the vegetables that have gone into it. You can't just eat the carrots. If you want the goodies, you've got to be willing to stir hard—and eat whatever it is your spoon brings up."

Sitting there in the hospital waiting room during my father's surgery, in the too-long moments I had to think about things, my spoon brought up many old feelings that had been ignored or forgotten. I had already confronted some of the hard things that needed to be said to my father and family, and celebrated joyful memories, too. But this was something different, a kind of diffuse sorrow for missed and blown opportunities that floated through my heart like dark clouds on a rainy day. Not all the doubts and regrets were big ones, although there were some. But under the glaring light of the hospital waiting room, things I hadn't even realized had sunk to the bottom of my bowl came up in my spoon.

I would have liked to talk about this with the friend who had given me so many gifts of wisdom over the years, not only advice about bowls of soup and crying Buddhas, but all of the everyday things good friends say to one another when they are part of each other's lives. But I could not tell her so. Somewhere along the line, some years after I moved away, we'd lost touch. I don't remember why. We just stopped calling and writing so much, and then, not at all. I felt somewhat betrayed, but guilty, too. I never had the chance to tell her good-bye. Maybe if we'd acknowledged that we were drifting? Called more often and spoke longer when we did? The last time I had sent a letter to my friend, it had come back to me "Addressee unknown: forwarding expired." That letter came up in my spoon, along with all kinds of omissions and commissions not thought about for years and years, and that suddenly seemed to be of vital, immediate importance.

Of course introspection and regret have their place. Sometimes, you come across things you can do something about, vowing to do better next time. Certainly, you learn from the things that happen to you and from your mistakes. But other times, when you find yourself dwelling only on your failures and regrets, this is a clue that you are only seeing half of the truth. I am reminded of a favorite story told about the famous rabbi, the Baal Shem Tov. A man of great devotion once approached the rabbi, saying, "I have labored hard and long to do my best to serve God with my life, and yet I have consistently fallen short of my goals. I am still an ordinary and ignorant person."

The Baal Shem Tov replied, "You have gained the realization that you are ordinary and ignorant, and this in itself is a worthy accomplishment."

The Baal Shem Tov reminds us that at times like this, it is incumbent upon you to think not only about your shortcomings but also to note all the good you have done, the progress you've made, the joy you've shared, the people you've touched. Perhaps you have not achieved every one of your goals—of course you haven't. No matter who you are, time is always too short and the task always too huge. But at the same time: Isn't it true that you are a little less crazy now than you used to be? Aren't you a little more willing to tell the truth than you once were? Don't you pay a little more attention to worthwhile things? And don't you have a little more compassion for yourself and for others?

Your life has been rich and full, offering you plenty of opportunities to grow your spirit. There have been moments of supreme happiness—and moments of angst. And you have learned from your trials and disappointments as well as from your triumphs. Not just once, but over and over again.

Life is ultimately too complicated for all of us; you are not alone when you weigh and measure your personal history, hoping to find that the good things outnumber the bad. At such moments, it is imperative that you not only tell the truth, but that you tell the whole truth. You have feared that you have sometimes been inadequate—but is it possible that you have set high standards for yourself, to stretch you beyond that to which you would not otherwise have aspired? You have bemoaned that you were overlooked—but is it possible that you have been left to ripen on the vine to be plucked when you have reached your fullest potential? You have feared that you have contributed to your own or to another's pain—but is it the depth of your relationships that makes you experience life so deeply?

Have you ached for life to feel whole again and feel that resolution is always just beyond your grasp? Remember that just as homesickness points to your experience of a real home, so does your yearning for resolution contain the memory of what has also already been yours.

46

It is your unrest itself that proclaims the truth that wholeness of spirit is real and possible. You can feel this way only because you know what connection to spirit means, and what it is to be fully alive. The greatness of your yearning gives testimony to the depth of your love. As the mystics teach: You would not seek if you had not already been found.

C. S. Lewis, the great Christian writer and polemicist, once told an illuminating story about his wife, Joy.

"Once, years ago, she was haunted one morning by a feeling that God wanted something of her, a persistent pressure like the nag of a neglected duty. And till midmorning she kept on wondering what it was. But the moment she stopped worrying, the answer came through as plain as a spoken voice. It was 'I don't want you to do anything. I want to give you something,' and immediately her heart was peace and delight."

ᴥ Come As You Are

You have only one sacred duty:

to make your spirit available to others.

You do this by sharing what you already are

in this and every moment.

If you are loving, you share your loving.

If you are suffering, you share your suffering.

If you are healing, you share your healing.

Why waste precious energy arguing with God about

what it is that is yours to share right now,

worrying how your broken bit could possibly be of

use.

Trust that however unlikely it may seem,

without your piece,

the universe would be incomplete.

∾ *Unbearable*

When you have really been through it,
 pummeled and raked,
 punctured and broken

And yet, you show up,
 still game
 ready to struggle for meaning

You are on the path that few walk by choice.
But the only way that leads to the genuine
 life of the spirit.

⌒ *Am I Making Progress?*

You don't need to know whether you are progressing
spiritually,
   increasing your enlightenment,
   improving your chances for heaven.

It is enough to love another
   and leave the rest to God.

◦ Miracles

Perhaps you are waiting for healing to come suddenly
    dramatic and sweeping,
    engulfing you in love.
And who is to say it won't happen like this?

But in the meantime,
    you can be a simple gardener
    tending your heart with love of your own.
No need to burn clear the ground
    for your garden is already growing
    and healing comes gently as you make room for new
      growth,
        simply by plucking out one weed at a time.

CHAPTER 6

Hope for Mortals

When You Fear That the Answer
to Your Prayer Is "No"

LEAP TO FAITH

While I watched the clock on the wall of the hospital waiting room slowly ticking away each minute of my father's operation, I found myself holding equal portions of hope and fear in my heart. Sometimes, my hope felt dishonest. Sometimes, my fear felt disloyal. Nor was I sure how to pray. Should I ask God to bring Dad back to us—or to release him from his pain?

These emotions were only heightened when, the day after the operation, he went into a coma. The coma did not lift that day, or the next. In fact, nearly a week dragged by. As nurses came in to tend his still body, Mom and I searched for the magic words that would awaken Dad from his relentless slumber. Sometimes we told stories, often we sang—favorite songs collected by Dad over the decades in yellowing notebooks I had stumbled across on his dresser. If only we could come up with just the right combination. "The clocks at home need winding," she'd say. "You know how much I love you, you know how

53

much I need you." Over and over again, she repeated these few simple phrases, an incantation delivered passionately, heart to heart.

I searched for words, too. "I'm here, Dad. I love you, Dad. Mom needs you to come back, Dad." But more than anything, I wanted to crawl into his arms, sobbing out what seemed to me to be the impossibly disloyal truth. I could not stand to see him like this, and after the weeks of physical suffering that I had witnessed him going through, I no longer had it in me to be brave. Maybe what he was waiting for was the one word we most resisted saying, *Good-bye.* God knows it wasn't what I wanted, but this situation couldn't be what he wanted, either—suspended between here and there. When Mom left the room for a short break, I whispered, *I want you to come back to us, healed and out of pain. I have hope that this is what will be. But at the same time, I release you, Dad. If you want to go, you need to know it's okay. I'll take care of Mom. I'll wind the clocks.*

From the moment I spoke my secret truth to Dad, the quality of light in the intensive care unit seemed to change. It was still dim, but warmer somehow. Suddenly, it was as if I had become aware of the presence of angels, standing with us at the side of Dad's bed, at his feet and head. The mysterious coma persisted; however, now there were subtle signs of progress. Sometimes when we spoke to him, his head turned in our direction, but his eyes were clouded, uncomprehending. Every once in awhile, Dad turned his head, as if straining to hear voices we could not.

I comforted myself with the thought that he was eavesdropping on the angels who were debating his situation, knowing full well that Dad listened in:

"There's his wife of more than seventy years, begging us to bring him back to her."

"But he's so old and so tired. You know he's prepared to go."

"Nobody who truly loves his or her life as much as this man does is ever truly prepared to go. He may accept that this is inevitable and be gracious or even relieved to surrender, but if he could stay, he would."

"And live a diminished life, a life in pain? Wouldn't it be better to let him fade into the light? Anyway, this is not a matter for the family to decide. This is between this man and God."

"So, should his family pray for him to live, or pray for him to be released from his suffering?"

"They should pray as we do: for God's will to be done."

For several days after I had whispered to Dad that he had my permission to go, I wondered if I had done the right thing.

It's not that I am a stranger to death, nor is it that death is my enemy. Some years before my father had faced a life-threatening illness, I had been diagnosed with my own: breast cancer. As I underwent a mastectomy and chemotherapy, I had plenty of time to think about dying. While many of the people who came to visit me related to my illness as if I had fallen into enemy hands, I instinctively found myself coming to terms with death not as the adversary, but as a natural if untimely part of life's rhythm. Ironically, many of my visitors viewed death as the destroyer of meaning. But on my side of the line, I began to view death not as a destroyer but rather as a creator of meaning. I treasured every moment, every exchange. The gift of a rose, the touch of a loved one's hand. Even the taste of water.

For me, facing my own mortality was transforming. Like my favorite midrash from the Jewish tradition, I identified with the Seraphim, angels in attendance to God whose only job it is to recite, "Holy, Holy, Holy," three times. They never make it all the way through their prayer, however, since halfway through the first *Holy,* they are so consumed by love, awe, and humility, they burn to ash. With this prayer, I could live with all my losses: a whole generation of relatives, the death of my beloved grandmothers, Dan's dad, birth mom, and brother, some very special friends, and our miscarried child.

It's not that I am *not* greedy for life—as much of it as I can cram into that little hyphen between the dates. I want to live fully every second of my allotted time, placing my bets on hope and miracles even when the outcome I prefer has no guarantees. Could my hope be mistaken? As long as whether hope is justified or not is even a question, I will take the risk of hoping that what I am praying for is still a real possibility.

And so, I am not afraid to ask God for exactly what I

want. *Ask* is perhaps an understatement. Okay, I am willing to yell at God. I negotiate. I beg. I pray. Sometimes I am Moses pleading with God to pick somebody else; sometimes I am Abraham bargaining fervently with the Almighty; and sometimes I am Jacob wrestling with God's agent on the riverbank, demanding that God give me a blessing.

I wanted desperately to hope for Dad, too, but every time Mom talked to Dad about needing him to come home and wind the clocks, I felt guilty because of what I had said, even if I had thought it was the right thing to say. But with six days of the coma passing, and all signs of progress apparently at a standstill, Mom became exhausted, too. Just before our lunch break, one of the intensive care nurses handed Mom a hospital directive to consider signing, having to do with restricting staff from performing extraordinary medical measures. It was as if the dam broke, and all the things that needed to be discussed—and that we had each resisted bringing up first—came tumbling out. We started talking about retirement homes where Mom could live near us. We spoke about cremation versus burial. We talked about practical matters, and we talked about matters of faith. We talked about everything, leaving nothing important unsaid. We did what we had to do, and it was all still hope. But it was hope for something new: that our faith in God would be justified, giving us a sense of peace and resolution, no matter what the outcome might be.

I struggled to do God's will—but how could I, a mere human, know without a doubt what God intended for me, for my mom and my dad? Even if I thought that we were doing the right thing discussing the practical ramifications of Dad's mortality, was I somehow contributing to the ultimate outcome, a kind of misguided prayer in reverse? But God reminded me once again that we human beings only think we have the power to call the shots.

When Mom and I returned to the intensive care unit after our lunch, for the first time, the curtains across the sliding glass door to Dad's room were drawn shut. Anxiously, we hurried inside.

There, lying on the bed, Dad turned to us and smiled.

"Hello, people!" he said weakly but distinctly. His gaze had cleared, too, and he and Mom locked eyes as if for the first time.

∽

We try so hard to believe that we are in control of our lives. Admitting helplessness is always a last resort. It is so hard to simply let yourself do the best you can—given the limitations of what it means to be a human being—and leave the rest to God.

This is the challenge a certain hiker faced one day. When walking along a steep mountain path, she slipped off the edge. By grabbing at the last moment onto an overhanging branch of a tree, she saved herself from a precipitous fall. And then, holding on for dear life hundreds of feet above the ground, the hiker heard the limb begin to crack.

This woman had never believed in God, but felt that this was as good a time as any to begin.

"God, are you up there?"

"Yes, my daughter," God replied. "What can I do for you?"

"God, help me. Tell me what to do!" she cried.

"You really want to know?"

The limb cracked a little more. Desperate, she cried out again.

"Yes, God. Tell me!"

There was a moment's silence. Then God answered her.

"Let go of the branch."

"Let go of the branch?"

"Yes, my daughter. Let go of the branch."

There was another moment's silence, then the hiker spoke.

"Is there anybody else up there?"

Of course it is all right to ask God for what you really want. We wish we never had to suffer or take the risk of hoping or to experience the pain of loss. We wish for stronger branches, lower mountain ridges, and steadier feet. Above all, we wish that life were easier—that it came with an owner's manual and money-back guarantees.

When circumstances force us to confront our ultimate helplessness, it takes a leap of faith to trust that God is present and loving, listening to our requests, watching over us. If we become frightened, angry, or frustrated, we can turn to God and ask to be shown whether there isn't something more we could be doing—or something we should stop doing. We can search our hearts for more humility or gratitude, for stronger faith.

But it may also be true that there is nothing more for us to say or do. At these times, we must consider the possibility that we may have already received the answer to our prayers—and the answer is, "no."

At these times, knowing this may be a possibility, how can we find the strength to face the challenges ahead?

Dealing with the ramifications of a severe stroke and related physical problems late in life, Ram Dass shared a story that had been inspirational to him. The story is about an army officer and a monk.

This particular army officer wasn't just any army officer. He was the most ferocious warrior in his land. As he led his soldiers through the countryside, he encouraged them to kill and pillage everyone and everything that crossed their path. Under his command, the soldiers were particularly harsh with the monks they encountered in monasteries along the way, not only humiliating the men of faith, but often putting them through horrible tortures.

When word arrived that the army officer and his soldiers had arrived in the town where one monastery in particular was located, all the monks but one fled. When the captain heard of this, he went directly to the monastery to confront the one monk who had dared to defy him. When he pushed open the gates, he saw the lone monk standing in the middle of the courtyard, watching him without any indication of fear. The captain approached him, asking in his most belligerent voice, "Don't you know who I am? I could take my sword and run it through your belly without blinking an eye!"

"And don't you know who I am?" replied the monk, gently. "I could have your sword run through my belly without blinking an eye."

Ram Dass concludes that the captain, recognizing the greater truth of the moment, sheathed his sword, bowed, and left.

∿ Earth and Ashes

Rabbi Bunan said to his disciples,
"Everyone must have two pockets,
    so that he can reach into the one or the other,
      according to his needs."

In his right pocket are to be the words:
    "For my sake was the world created."
In his left:
    "I am earth and ashes."

∿ *While We Wait*

While We Wait

> we hope for bliss to envelop us,
>
> taking away our sadness and pain.

The light should grow brighter

> and beautiful music fill the air,
>
> angels to appear
>
> and magic hands come to heal.

But while we wait, yet can we practice kindness.

> We can love.
>
> We can serve.
>
> We can forgive.

Nothing out of the ordinary,

> yet God's greatest gifts.

∽ I'm Confused

Dear God,

Help me to remember that the outcome I desire is not
only up to me.

I admit I'm sometimes confused and don't always know
what's right

or best for me to do.

Remind me that, in truth,

I don't need to know what it's all about.

It's job enough for me right now

to keep putting one foot ahead of the other.

Grant me patience,

as the unfolding processes of time

illuminate the decisions I need to make,

the words I need to speak.

Amen.

∾ *Be with Us*

God, some of us are angry with you!
Be with us, anyway.

God, some of us are afraid we've failed you.
Be with us, anyway.

God, some of us ask how we can put our faith in you
    in face of all that we are enduring.
Be with us, anyway.

God, some of us don't believe in you any more.
Be with us, anyway.

∿ Where Is God?

Sometimes it feels as though the boat were breaking up
  beneath us
    as we row for shore.

Is this a time to push or a time to rest?
    To persevere or to let go?
    To fight or to surrender?

The answer will come more readily when we remember
  this:

God is not only the shore,
    but the ocean.

CHAPTER 7

Sacred Space

When There Are No Words That Will Suffice

SIMPLY PRESENT

The story is told of the Chinese philosopher Lao-tzu that he once turned to his students and asked them, "Which of you knows the fragrance of a rose?"

When they all nodded in affirmation, Lao-tzu continued. "Put it into words."

All of them were silent.

Sometimes we search for the right words to say, but it is as if we have jumped into the ocean at its deepest place. We find ourselves swimming downward into the darkness. Our failure to find words to express our feelings exposes mysteries beyond comprehension. It brings us to the same humbled place to which Trappist monk and writer Thomas Merton arrived through his studies of the Bible where he discovered "the strange and paradoxical world of meanings and experiences that are beyond us and yet often extremely and mysteriously relevant to us."

Sometimes, we must confront the possibility that there are simply no words that will suffice. When we find ourselves speechless, we can give up the struggle to understand, explain, or talk it away. When we have exhausted our possibilities, that is the exact moment when God reaches out to us and cradles our fall. This is sacred space, exquisite and complete: a place where we can at last collapse into God's warm embrace and allow ourselves to be still.

After sitting vigil many nights with a loved one, writer Michael Downey explained that to have been able to offer the gift of simple presence at a time of need "seems to me to have been the one thing for which I was created—love, itself."

How easy it is to fear that we have disappointed others by failing to do great things. We struggle to find the words to say and to hear words that hold important meaning. But in his simple wisdom, Michael teaches us that only one thing really matters: "To do little things with great love."

Sometimes, we find ourselves facing questions to which we can find no response. As deep as you've gone, go deeper yet. Do not fear the silence. Words at their best contain the wisdom of humanity, while silence embraces us with the abundance of God.

❧ Something Special

How we have longed to be someone in the world:
>   to be special,
>   above the rest,
>   looked up to,
>   above reproach,
>   lauded and praised.

Perhaps we have penetrated these dizzying heights,
>   perhaps only dreamt of our elevated destiny.

In sacred space, we learn that special is also apart,
>   above is also separate,
>   and dizzying heights a lonely place to live.

And so we descend,
>   only to discover that someone has been there all
>   along,
>   waiting for us with open arms.

∿ Search for the Perfect Gift

I want to give you flowers,

    but there's something more.

I want to give you a meaningful card,

    but there's something more.

I want to find exactly the right words,

    but there's something more.

I want to give you the world,

    but there's something more.

I want to give you the impulse in my heart

    that moves me to show you how much I care.

And that's all that matters.

Don't Injure Yourself

You stand guard through the night
    pushing yourself to stay awake.

You wish you could do more,
    but in your heart,
you know that to pay heed to this call
    is to exceed your capacity.

So understand this:
    God does not want you to injure yourself doing
    God's work.
When you are exhausted, go to sleep
    and trust God to do God's work.

❦ *Precious Breath*

In sacred space, there is so very little separating our
   hearts from the divine.
Each breath, no matter how halting,
      has strength enough to flutter aside the gossamer
      curtains
      and let more of God's love in.

∿ Finding the Words

Suffering frees us to set aside our everyday words
and to huddle together in silence.

Why struggle to find just the right thing to say
and yearn for verbal keepsakes?

Rest, instead, in the sacred space beyond words,
where love and wisdom can not be captured,
only lived.

Part I Postscript

One More Thing . . .

Dad's recovery was long and difficult. He was in rehabilitation at the hospital for nearly a month. He'd
lost thirty pounds, and his clothes hung on him. But bit by
bit, he started to come back. His sense of humor returned
first, long before his strength. When his voice was still
slurred, not more than a whisper, Mom and I bent close to
him, to catch every word. He hadn't eaten for two weeks,
tubes with various colored liquids sustained him. "Bring
me a piece of cardboard," he whispered. "Cardboard?" we
replied. "Yes, I need to make a sign: *Will Work for Food.*"
Before long, he was sitting up in a chair in the room, eat-
ing meatloaf and carrots. Then he began to walk. He even
started to sing again.

When at last he was released to return home, Mom and
Dad had to deal with home health and unwanted medical
apparatus, negotiating public transportation after a lifetime
behind the wheel. At first I pushed for the folks to move
close to me, then when I saw how well they were doing
overall, I changed my mind, to everybody's relief. In the
middle of everything, my brother and I had a ridiculous

fight, but we made up. Because you have troubles of your own, I won't fill you in on every detail. Suffice it to say that just when I thought I'd said everything that would or could ever need to be said, suddenly, when I thought that I was completely at peace with Dad and my family and that our relationship was healed and whole, there was one more thing.

Maybe there's always one more thing. I mean, we try so hard to get it right and sometimes, it still doesn't turn out the way we think it should. Sometimes circumstances make it impossible to get in that final word we hope will bring us peace and completion. And sometimes too, things are said, often under the stresses of the moment or under the influence of pain or medication, that are taken far too seriously. Confusing things. Hurtful things.

Sometimes we don't get the opportunity to respond, to clarify, to resolve. And sometimes we do, and say the wrong thing anyway.

Sometimes we don't even know the darkness we are harboring inside, catching mere glimpses of phantom shadows that find clever ways to elude expression. Other times we find the courage to reach out and catch the darkness, only to recognize that the thing we find is still too vulnerable to expose to the world.

I'm not sure how or why it is that I came through this long, trying time with one more thing left to say. God knows, I had plenty of opportunities to talk to Dad. I thought I'd said everything. While he was in the hospital, we'd talked about things we hoped to do together when he got well and what I should do with my life in case he did not. We talked about my strengths and my not-so-strengths, and he shared his hopes for me and my family.

And despite this, if Dad had died, the one thing more I never said could have seemed bigger to me than all the rest put together. Forget all the stories and singing, the hand-holding and earnest conversations. The one more thing was in danger of becoming the only thing.

But Dad didn't die. And for all of us who have lost people for whom we've cared deeply, haunted by the one thing that needed to be said, I share with you what happened next.

When the doctors finally set a release date for Dad to come home, I wanted to be there to help out. The transition was going to be a tricky one, integrating health care workers and new medical routines into Mom and Dad's world.

And I wanted to be there to bring about a sense of completion to this episode in all our lives.

And then, there was the matter of the something left unsaid. By the time I was on the plane to Los Angeles, I knew the exact words I was going to have to find the courage to say, and I knew exactly how it would feel to say them. Terrible. But say them, I must.

It took awhile to find the right time. I couldn't do it that first day, when Dad was running through the apartment like a happy puppy. Nor the second, when the complexities of his new life became a more sober reality. But on the third day, I suddenly realized that Mom was out back doing the laundry and Dad was alone, reading the newspaper.

"Dad, there's something I feel terrible about. Something I need to ask your forgiveness for. Do you remember when I came to visit last year on my book tour? You were going to accompany me to a speech I had been asked to give in a town nearby. You said you knew how to get there and that we were leaving in plenty of time. I asked if I should get directions. You said it wasn't necessary. And I wanted to drive the car, but you wouldn't let me. And then we got lost. Remember? We had no idea where we were, and it was just a few minutes before my speech was supposed to start. Well, the thing is, I'm so sorry I screamed at you. Can you ever forgive me?"

Dad looked at me with a funny expression on his face.

"You screamed at me? I don't remember that."

"The scream, Dad! It was terrible. How could you forget?"

Sometime during our exchange, Mom had come back into the living room and had been quietly listening in. She could no longer restrain herself.

"Have you forgotten something, Carol? Dad is stone deaf in his right ear. He never heard a thing."

"That couldn't be. You must have heard me, Dad. It was
78   really, truly terrible!"

I searched his eyes for the truth, and the bemused expression that I found there told me everything.

He never even knew.

Even though Dad had not even heard me yell at him, he forgave me anyway. Not because he needed to, but because I needed him to.

The day my plane was scheduled to leave, I was sitting alone in the living room. It was early morning, and the sun was streaming into the room. There were no shadows. I heard footsteps behind me, but before I could turn around, Dad was bending over, kissing me on the top of my head.

"This is for nothing," he said.

Then it was time to go.

~

Sometime after I'd returned home from Mom and Dad's house, I realized that I no longer had any idea where the crying Buddha that my friend had given me ten years ago now was. After writing about it, thinking about it, taking comfort from the memory of it, it was gone.

At first, I was upset about the loss. The crying Buddha had been my guide through rough times. It had taught me many lessons about life. Then, looking at the emptiness on my bedside table where I would have liked the little statue to be, I realized that the crying Buddha's course of learning was nearly complete. Rivers of sadness and love had done their work, carving ravines in my heart. Within me, there were now deep channels of emotion I knew would be with me the rest of my life. I felt love and life flowing through me, strong and steady. But before I was able to complete this chapter of my life, there was one last lesson left for me to master.

Turning toward the emptiness, I remembered the rest of the crying Buddha's lesson. You see, the point of healing is not about being any one way: not only happy, but not only sad, either. The key to living a full life is to become willing to embrace it all.

And then, at last, came the joy.

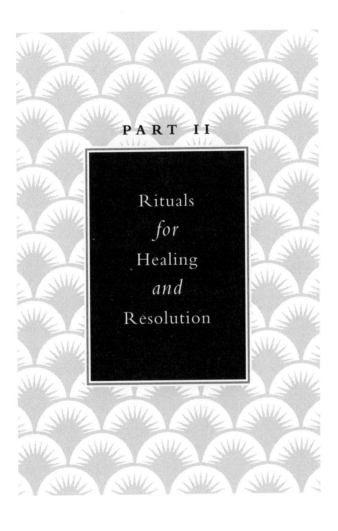

PART II

Rituals
for
Healing
and
Resolution

∾ Take the One Seat

Buddhist teacher and author Jack Kornfield shares a powerful ritual that his teacher Achaan Chah taught him. In the ritual he calls "Taking the One Seat," you are advised to take a seat in the center of a room, open all the doors and windows, and see who comes to visit. "You will witness all kinds of scenes and actors, all kinds of temptations and stories, everything imaginable. Your only job is to stay in your seat. You will see it all arise and pass, and out of this, wisdom and understanding will come."

If you can't put a seat in the center of a room, a hospital bed or even a centrally located chair in a waiting area can provide you with an adequate vantage point from which to view the drama of life as it unfolds about you. Recline or sit in as relaxed a manner as possible, slowing down your breathing and opening your heart to compassionately embrace whatever happens to cross your path. People may come and go, bringing with them all manner of busyness, news, stories, and moods. You may encounter sadness, fear, desire, anger, frustration, or shame—but you may also come in contact with compassion, happiness, love, and resolution. Be open to whatever comes your way. As you are able and willing, silently offer a simple blessing with each new person, situation, thought, or feeling that arises. You could say something to yourself along the lines of "Bless this crying child," "Bless this bossy nurse," "Bless this fear," and so on.

Continue this ritual of acceptance and compassion for as long as you wish.

∾ Tell God How You Really Feel

Find your first opportunity to tell God exactly how you feel about what you are going through. If to communicate your feelings honestly you have to wail or scream, find a private place where you can really let go. Alone in a car provides a good place to release your pent-up emotions. If you are really self-conscious, drive to a secluded area—like the far end of a shopping center or hospital parking lot—and turn your radio up as loud as possible. If you can't get away, don't worry. You don't even have to speak your grievances out loud. God reads your heart long before the words leave your lips.

Whether you find yourself whispering or shouting, by addressing your grievances to God, you make your feelings potent. Tempered by divine compassion, the sharp edges round and soften. Infinite grievance turns into infinite compassion. Your justified complaints will empower rather than deplete you.

∾ Listen with an Open Heart

This is perhaps the simplest ritual, but sometimes the most difficult to do. Simply listen to another person, without judgment, resistance, or fear. Put your complete attention on the other's full communication—not just the words, but also the tone, the facial expression, the body movement. See if you can really tune in, without worrying or thinking through what your reply should be, what you should say next.

If you are concerned about what you might hear, feel, or project, envision a protective screen between you and the other, filtering out that which is troublesome, allowing through only that which is good and loving.

∾ Share Your Story

You and your loved one have lived through challenging times before. There was the destiny of your birth, which placed you with a certain family and in particular circumstances, and there were the important people who came in and out of your life. There were the tragedies that dulled the edges of your arrogance, giving you depth and compassion. There were brave choices and poor decisions. Arguments and reconciliation. Things happened to you that you could not possibly have anticipated. Certainly there were mistakes you made that you never need make again. The one for whom you care so deeply made mistakes, as well.

But you have had wonderful things happen to you, too: twists and turns of fate that sent you off on adventures you could not have anticipated. In fact, if you were to put the events of your life together in the hands of a great storyteller, you would soon see yourselves as the protagonists of a wonderful tale. And why not? This is your opportunity.

First, think of a good title for your story, something that captures the flavor of this important relationship in your life.

Next, identify three or so turning points in your relationship. What are the three most important events in your life together to date? Once you have your list of the three most important events, here are some suggested topics to discuss or think about in relation to each turning point.

1. What is a particular memory from that time of our lives that captures the flavor of my experience?

2. Could we have done anything more or different about our situation, given the circumstances we faced, where we came from, and what we knew then?

3. How does the situation that happened at that time relate to what I am feeling today?

4. What do we know now that we didn't know then?

The ancient Hebrews used the same word for spirit as they did for breath: *Ruach.*Check your breathing right now. At the time we most need unobstructed access to our spirit, our breath becomes rapid and shallow instead of full and deep.

Here's a simple practice that will help you to breathe deeply, and at the same time, to use your breath as a powerful tool of transformation.

Start by thinking of some quality you would like to reduce in your life right now. Perhaps you would like to give up the fear that you won't have enough time to say everything that needs to be said, or whatever else you wish you could let go. Then think of a quality you would like more of in your life, and summarize it with a single word: *faith, compassion,* and so on. For our example, we will use the pair of *fear* and *peace.*

Now, start by breathing in. Make it a deep, slow breath, and as you do, think to yourself, "I welcome peace." When you have breathed in as deeply as possible, gently release your breath completely, thinking to yourself, "I let go of fear." Do this for as long as it is helpful to you.

∿ Journey to Healing

When you take a well-deserved break, you can go on a symbolic journey to revive your spirit as well as your body.

Your travels can remain indoors, wandering about hallways and waiting rooms, or take you outside. As you go, hold this question in mind: "What do I need to heal?" Then, as you stroll, keep yourself receptive to personally meaningful signs in the environment. Be open to anything that speaks to you.

It may be a tender new sprout growing out of the blackened stump of a tree, a drinking fountain that is always flowing with cool water, or a fire hydrant that appears to be standing bravely, arms outstretched, as if saluting you. Make note of each stop you make along the way, and think of a simple response. To the tender sprout, you may want to put your hand over your heart and send it love. To the water fountain, you may enjoy taking a sip you know is helping you to heal. To the brave little hydrant, you may want to pause and salute back. By keeping a mental note of your stops, you can repeat the ritual journey again and again.

Each time you do, the healing rituals become more and more potent. You anticipate reaching each station as you would an old friend. Your breaks become spiritually healing, as you take sacred geography into your life.

॰ Forgive the Past

The Buddhist tradition gives us a powerful ritual of forgiveness that extends release from blame and regret we have held against others who have hurt us, others we have hurt, and finally, transgressions we have committed against ourselves. You can do this ritual by reading the instructions to yourself and then closing your eyes to deepen your experience; or you can guide another through it by reading each of the instructions aloud, pausing frequently so that they may experience the process fully.

The tradition teaches that forgiveness may not be instantaneous but is a practice that may require ongoing dedication. Persist, and you will receive one of the greatest gifts of spiritual life. As Jack Kornfield writes, "You will see that forgiveness is fundamentally for your own sake, a way to carry the pain of the past no longer. The fate of the person who harmed you, whether they be alive or dead, does not matter nearly as much as what you carry in your heart. And if the forgiveness is for yourself, for your own guilt, for the harm you've done to yourself or to another, the process is the same. You will come to realize that you can carry it no longer."

The formal forgiveness meditation, adapted for our purposes from Jack Kornfield's book, *A Path with Heart,* begins by asking you to sit or lie down in a comfortable position, letting your eyes close gently, and allowing your breath to flow in and out easily and naturally. When you are relaxed, let yourself feel the burden of not yet having forgiven others or yourself, or the weight of not having been forgiven by others.

When you have a general sense of the heaviness in your heart, turn your thoughts in turn to each of the three categories of forgiveness, saying these words, as shared by Jack Kornfield, either to yourself or out loud.

FOR FORGIVENESS FROM OTHERS

There are many ways that I have hurt and harmed others, betrayed or abandoned them, caused them suffering, knowingly or unknowingly, out of my pain, fear, anger, and confusion.

After you have spoken these words, think about the many ways and times you have hurt others. Experience the pain you caused and your own sadness and regret. When you have fully addressed each memory and sense that you are ready to release this burden, say these words:

I ask for your forgiveness.

Then turn your attention to the next memory that comes up for you, and keep repeating the process until you have asked forgiveness from others for everything that comes to mind.

When you have completed this first part of the ritual, you are ready to begin part 2.

For Forgiveness for Yourself

This time, think about all the ways you have hurt or injured yourself, saying these words:

> *There are many ways that I have betrayed, harmed,*
> *or abandoned myself through thought, word, or deed,*
> *knowingly or unknowingly.*

Feel the burden of your regret, thinking of specific times, instances, and ways you have harmed yourself. When you sense that you are ready to forgive yourself, say these words:

> *For each of the ways I have hurt myself through*
> *action or inaction, out of my fear, pain, and confu-*
> *sion, I now extend a full and heartfelt forgiveness. I*
> *forgive myself.*

For Forgiveness for Those Who Have Hurt or Harmed You

Begin by saying these words:

> *There are many ways I have been wounded and*
> *hurt, abused and abandoned, by others in thought,*
> *word, or deed, knowingly or unknowingly.*

Remember these injustices, feeling the grief you have carried with you from your past. When you sense that you can release each burden, one by one, say to yourself:

In the many ways others have hurt or harmed me, out of fear, pain, confusion, and anger, I see these now. To the extent that I am ready, I offer them forgiveness. I have carried this pain in my heart too long. For this reason, to those who have caused me harm, I offer you my forgiveness. I forgive you.

When you open your eyes, you will feel a newfound softness in your heart and the sense that you are being released from regret.

Wash Away Fear and Anger

The next time you wash your hands, imagine all your fears, angers, and concerns flowing down into your fingers. Now wash your hands and imagine the soap and water washing away everything you no longer need or want. When you are done, let the cool water flow over your hands for awhile longer, taking as long as you need to feel cleansed and renewed.

∾ Remember God

It is easy in the stresses of life to sometimes forget about God. But know this: God is with you always, whether you are thinking about God or not. In God, there is abundant love and forgiveness. You can bring your cares and concerns to God, and rest in God's comforting embrace.

Sometimes, it helps us to have reminders of this. So choose something repetitive in your life right now—the sound of a nurse's bell chiming in the distance, a stoplight, a cup of coffee, whatever comes to mind. Now, every time you encounter this signal, take a moment to remember God.

❧ Clarify Your Thoughts

When we are under pressure, unformed feelings may surface that we cannot quite grasp. At exactly the same moment when we may be expected to think clearly, to make decisions, to tap into our own intuitive knowing, we may feel unfocused and confused. This writing exercise helps you pierce through the fogginess and put you in touch with what is really going on with you.

For the next ten minutes, write nonstop, never taking the pen off the paper, except for between words and when you turn the page. Write as fast as you can. Write anything that comes into your mind. But here's the thing: Don't lead your thoughts, follow them. For instance, you might start out thinking about a decision you have to make, and then suddenly, a thought about someone you love intervenes. Follow this thought until it, too, is interrupted by another thought and so on. This takes discipline and honesty. For instance, if you are struck for something to say, write, "I am stuck, I am still stuck, this is stupid how stuck I am," and so on, following whatever words come into your own mind. If you are still blocked, or feel that no matter how much you'd like to, you can't get your worrying, goal-setting, rational mind out of the way, switch your pen to your less dominant hand. Write about how hard it feels to write with your other hand. Write down that thought—that thought—that thought. Let mistakes go uncorrected. Keep writing nonstop, the whole ten minutes.

Before long, your writing will naturally and effortlessly lead you deeper and deeper. Eventually, you will find yourself caught up in a flow of wise and true thoughts, providing you with increased clarity and perspective about the real issues in your life.

∼ Communicate with Touch

There are many versions of healing touch. But one of the most effective is also the simplest. Stand or sit near someone who is in need of healing. Close your eyes and put your hands over your heart. Feel love for the person and let the energy of your love warm your hands. When your hands feel warm and tingly, take your hands and place them lightly on the one for whom you care. If it is not possible to actually touch the person, you can place your hand a few inches above their body or simply imagine doing so. Now imagine that through your hands you are transferring the energy of love, healing, and peace into the one for whom you care.

~ Call on an Archangel for Strength

Mystics in the Jewish tradition have a powerful ritual, to be used only when the need is great.

If this is such a moment for you, sit or stand in as balanced a way as possible. Check to see that your weight is evenly distributed and that you are steady. Hold onto something for support, if necessary.

Now ask the Archangel Michael to make himself known to you, to give you the loving strength and protection you need. Imagine the archangel walking up behind you and placing his strong hands gently but firmly on your shoulders. Now imagine him standing there with you, his large white wings opening and closing in a slow, deliberate rhythm behind your back. Know that he will stay with you as long as you need him.

❧ Center Yourself in Prayer

This Centering Prayer is inspired by Father Thomas Keating, a Cisterian priest, monk, and abbot. It begins with your selection of a sacred word or phrase—any word or phrase that expresses to you your experience of a power greater than yourself. It may be *God, Loving Universe,* or *Peace,* or any other word or phrase that reminds you of your willingness to engage with the divine.

Keating writes, "The word is a sacred word because it is a symbol of your intention to open yourself to the mystery of God's presence beyond thoughts, images, or emotions. It is chosen not for its content but for its intent. It is merely a pointer that expresses the direction of your inner movement toward the presence of God."

After you have your sacred word in mind, find the best place for this ritual to transpire. If possible, find a quiet spot where you can be alone. You may not have a choice about this if you need to stay in a hospital room or find yourself reading this in a crowded airport terminal. Just do the best you can.

The next step is to imagine a circle of light surrounding you. Now relax your eyes, closing them if you can. Focus your complete attention on the sacred word you have chosen. If your meditation is interrupted, revisit your word as soon and as often as you can—eyes opened or closed—and you will find it to be a spontaneous reminder of your connection to the divine.

❧ Write a Letter and Let It Go

When you yearn to say something to someone who for any reason cannot or will not be able to hear what you want to say to him or her, there is still something you can do. Write that person a letter. Don't hold anything back. Say everything that's in your mind and heart, as honestly and deeply as possible. When you are through, you can keep the letter with you for as long as it takes while you decide what to do with it. Sooner or later, you will know. If you find yourself ready to let it go, make a ritual of its release: burn it with a match in an ashtray, throw it into rushing water, tuck it in the uneaten pudding for the orderly to clear away, or think of your own special form of deliverance.

∿ *Comfort Your Pain*

Imagine any emotional or physical pain you are feeling to be a small child who is crying to you for help. Now take the child in your arms, and comfort your pain. If you'd like, rock gently back and forth, or sing the child a soothing song.

∾ Walk to Rejuvenate

Perhaps you know that taking a walk would be good for you, but you have found it hard to tear yourself away from your concerns. Here's a simple ritual that will allow you to take your thoughts and emotions with you, and to transform them into healing.

Before you start out on your walk, think of two qualities that would be helpful to you right now. Perhaps the qualities are love and faith, or patience and perseverance. Now assign one of these qualities to each of your feet. Perhaps love is your left foot and faith is your right. Now take a deep breath and start walking slowly and deliberately. Each time your left foot connects with the ground, think "Love," each time your right foot connects, think "Faith." Feel the earth rising up to greet each step, pouring the quality you are most in need of into you through the souls of your shoes. Take as long a walk as you can.

❧ Fix a Broken Record

Sometimes we become prisoners of repetitive thoughts or stories. The source of these relentless patterns may come from outside ourselves: someone who is dwelling nonstop on past injustices, unresolved issues, or worries about the future. Sometimes, the repeating story is in our own minds, running again and again nonproductively over the same tired ground.

If this is happening to you, whether the source is inside or outside your body, turn your attention to your physical responses to it. Do you feel your cheeks heating up? Is your stomach clenched? Identify the dominant sensation associated with the repetition of the thought or story, and give it a descriptive name. Perhaps you can call it "burning," or "pressure," or whatever word comes to mind.

The next time you find yourself responding negatively to this repetitive pattern, recognize the sensation by name: "Ah—there's burning, again." Then, while repeating the word over and over again—"Burning, burning, burning"— open yourself to any memories, images, or emotions that may spontaneously arise. Stay with it, and you will have the opportunity to witness the sensation spontaneously transform itself, revealing deeper and more productive layers of emotion. The burning feeling associated with a repetitive pattern may become anger, and anger may become grief. When you have reached your deepest emotion, you will begin to experience it as something that is healing rather than destructive. When the sensation is fully revealed to you, you will feel released.

❧ Keep Your Spirit Up

Often when we are under stress, our minds automatically think of the worst outcome possible of the situation we face.

It is helpful to remember, at these times, that the best outcome is possible, also.

Here is a simple way to create the optimum environment for healing to take place.

Close your eyes, if you can, and imagine that you and the one for whom you care are together in a small square of sacred space. Imagine that at each of the square's four corners there is a full, healthy rose bush in full bloom. Pick any color roses you'd like. Beneath you are rose petals of the same color. Now, pay attention to the rose bushes. If they start to wilt or droop, imagine them renewing themselves. When they are full and healthy, you can open your eyes, keeping the feeling with you. Now, if and as worrisome thoughts occur to you, as people come and go and interactions and events transpire, remember every once in awhile to check on the state of your roses. If they are drooping, close your eyes again and repeat the process.

∼ Send Love Heart to Heart

Here is a powerful ritual that will allow you to give the gift of healing love to one for whom you care. The one you love can be with you, inches away, on the other side of the world, or only in your memories and dreams.

Relax into a comfortable position. If possible, close your eyes. Now, imagine a beam of loving light coming into you through the top of your head and into your heart. Feel your heart fill with light and love. Imagine the beam of light leaving your heart and entering your loved one's heart. Feel the warm and healing energy of the connection. As long as you remember to keep replenishing yourself with the infinite source of light and love, you can do this ritual as long and as often as you wish.

∽ Name Your Relationship

Every relationship has its own, unique name. Some relationships are "love," some are "compassion," some are "best friends." Even difficult relationships have provided opportunities for you to develop qualities you might not otherwise have developed in your life: "patience," "righteous anger," or "justice," among many other possibilities. Each one of these qualities is a shorthand way to think about the positive role a relationship has played in your life.

So, think about a relationship you'd like to heal right now. Ask yourself, What is this relationship's name? Every time you think about that relationship, even if your thoughts are difficult ones, remember to call it by name.

❧ *Take Spiritual Inventory*

If you are asking questions of meaning, feeling the presence of diffuse, unexpressed feelings about life in general and your life in particular, you may benefit from a spiritual inventory.

To undertake a spiritual inventory, follow these three steps.

1. Review key memories in your life with as little judgment as possible, beginning with reflection upon your earliest times. Trust that the most important memories for you to think about right now are the ones that will most readily occur to you.

2. As each memory comes to mind, simply ask yourself, What happened? Who were the key players? What happened as a result of the incident in your life and in the lives of others?

3. Each time you think of something pleasant, say a prayer of gratitude to God. Each time you think of something in need of healing or forgiveness, ask God to show you the way to rectify the situation. If there is nothing now to be done, let it go. If there is something you can do, do it now.

∿ Watch the Clouds

Ram Dass shares a powerful meditation ritual with us. Simply look out the window, or if you can, go outside, and watch the clouds go by.

Notice how the sky does not hold onto any one cloud. Nor do the clouds themselves feel obliged to hold to the same shape. By watching the clouds move across the sky, we can be inspired to bring this same quality of acceptance to our own lives.

∿ Embrace Your Highest Love

Remember a moment when you felt complete, unconditional love in your life. Close your eyes, and recreate that moment with as much detail as possible. Are there sounds or music associated with that moment? Special scents? Tactile sensations? Feelings?

When the memory is complete, imaging filling your heart with it. When you open your eyes, the facts and details of the memory will be gone, but the feelings will remain with you.

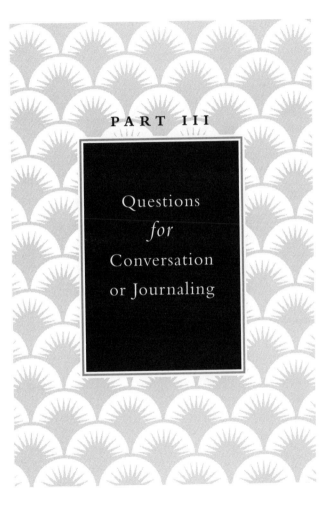

PART III

Questions
for
Conversation
or Journaling

Ask the Right Questions

Bedside vigils, long hours spent in hospital waiting rooms, and times of life transition can be portals to deeper conversation and connection with the people we love and with our own inner wisdom. When we find ourselves existing in extraordinary time, often we can access new levels of permission to say what needs to be said, hear what needs to be heard. Sometimes all we need is the right question to unlock the door.

You may use this carefully crafted list of questions in whatever way is most helpful to you. The questions have been organized in a gentle progression; however, feel free to skip ahead to those questions that speak to you and to pass on those that don't. There are at least three ways to use these questions.

The first suggestion is to use the questions as conversation starters with the person for whom you care. If your loved one is open to it, posing these questions can create an environment that allows you to gently address deeper issues that need to be accessed and healed. You might start with the first question and continue on through the list to its conclusion, as time and energy allow. If it feels right, you and your loved one might take turns answering the questions. Whether you are talking or listening, try to keep your heart open. You can most readily accomplish this by making room for the entire range of emotions, remembering that laughter and sadness, joy and sorrow, anger and forgiveness often come to us deeply intertwined. And remember, too, that being open and honest doesn't always mean you need to say or hear everything. Sometimes, the honest response is to admit to yourself that you must call upon your wisdom and maturity to keep some things to (or from) yourself. If the questions lead you into vulnerable areas, you can imagine surrounding you a filter that allows in or out only that which will be beneficial to you.

Take your time, trusting that the process of coming toward one another is more important than any particular result. You may well find your answers, the quality of your conversation, and your capacity to take things in without judgment deepen as you go.

Second, you can use these questions to pass time with family and friends during those long hours of waiting. These questions can open doors for you, and you will come to understand that even the most difficult of times can be transformed into sacred space when hearts make the sincere effort to reach out toward one another. If you're not used to talking with one another in such depth, turn the questions into a game, and trust that what is perfect for you and for those with whom you share this experience will unfold naturally, as it is meant to be.

114 Finally, you can use these questions to inspire your thoughts when journaling. In progression, the questions

move you deeper and deeper as you proceed through the list. Remember that there is no right or wrong answer to any of these questions. Be kind to yourself.

∾

1. When people speak highly of you, what do they say?

2. What has life taught you that you'd like to share with the people you love?

3. Do you believe in miracles?

4. What fear would you most like to get beyond?

5. What feelings come up for you when you think about God? If it were acceptable to be angry or upset, what would you say to God?

6. How many times a day would you like to be told that you are loved?

7. If you could relive one day of your life, which would you choose and why?

8. If you have a favorite song, what is it? If not, pick one now. Can you sing any of it? Hum the tune?

9. Do you remember a time when you felt particularly close to a loving presence greater than yourself? How about now?

10. What are the most loving things people have said or done about what you are going through? The stupidest or least sensitive?

11. Has anyone important to you ever asked you to forgive them for something? How did this impact how you felt about them?

12. If there were something you could rectify, what would it be?

13. If God wanted to lift God's spirits, what page of your life would God turn to first?

14. Do you believe it would be possible for anyone to live their life with no regrets?

15. If God gave you the job of making heaven, what would you create?

16. Which has contributed more to the growth of your character and your spirit: your successes or your disappointments?

17. What is something important you have no doubts about?

18. Is there someone whom you are prepared to forgive who might be surprised by your forgiveness?

19. Do the people in your life really know what you care most about?

20. What book do you wish everyone you care about would read?

21. What would you like others to know about you that you've never shared before?

22. What doubts, fears, or concerns do you have about death?

23. When was the last time you laughed so hard you started to cry?

24. If your physician has told someone you trust important information about your situation and is leaving it to them whether to share it with you or not, would you want them to share it with you or not?

25. What are you curious about?

26. What was one of the nicest things anyone has ever said to you about yourself?

27. If somebody wanted to make a film about your life, whom would you like them to cast in the leading role? Who should play supporting parts?

28. If there were one quality you'd like more of in your life, what would it be?

29. What haven't you said that you wish you could?

30. What haven't you heard that would be important for you to hear?

What do you need to say?

What do you need to hear?

Acknowledgments

My deepest gratitude goes to the many people who have encouraged me, not only in the writing of this book but in the living of my life.

To my agent and my friend, Linda Roghaar, for persisting with this project of love.

To Leslie Berriman, my editor, Heather McArthur, Sharon Donovan, Brenda Knight, Teresa Coronado, Leah Russell, Rosie Levy, Jenny Collins, Pam Suwinsky, Suzanne Albertson, and the extraordinary team of inspired professionals at Conari Press.

To those in my life recently passed on: Irene Rowland, Harry Rowland, Rose Kaplow, Ruth Sweet, and Nancy Askew, and the children—my friends and family—who remember you with love.

To the dedicated physicians, staffs, and certain generous visitors at Saddleback Memorial Hospital in Laguna Woods, California, and Vanderbilt University Medical center in Nashville, Tennessee. You had just the right words for a

121

stranger on those tender occasions when she was alone and in need.

And finally, to my husband, Dan, my children, Grant and Jody, and my parents, Mae and Lloyd. As always and forever, you are my greatest blessings.

Sources and Recommended Reading

Barks, Coleman, translator. *The Essential Rumi*. Edison, New
Jersey: Castle Books, 1997.

Joan Borysenko. *Pocketful of Miracles: Prayers, Meditations and
Affirmations to Nurture Your Spirit Every Day of the Year*.
New York: Warner Books, 1994.

Breton, Denise, and Christopher Largent. *Love, Soul and
Freedom: Dancing with Rumi on the Mystic Path*. Center
City, Minnesota: Hazelden, 1998.

Caplan, Mariana. *Halfway Up the Mountain: The Error of
Premature Claims to Enlightenment*. Prescott, Arizona:
Hohm Press, 1999.

Chödrön, Pema. *Start Where You Are: A Guide to Compassionate
Living*. Boston: Shambhala Publications, 1994.

Citron, Sterna. *Why the Baal Shem Tov Laughed: Fifty-Two
Stories about Our Great Chasidic Rabbis*. Northvale, New
Jersey: Jason Aronson, 1993.

Dosick, Wayne. *When Life Hurts: A Book of Hope*. San
Francisco: HarperSanFrancisco, 1998.

Kornfield, Jack. *A Path with Heart: A Guide through the Perils and Promises of Spiritual Life.* New York: Bantam Books, 1993.

Kroeber, Theodora. *Ishi in Two Worlds.* Berkeley, California: University of California Press, 1969.

Kuner, Susan, et al. *Speak the Language of Healing: Living With Breast Cancer Without Going to War.* Berkeley: Conari Press, 1999.

Kushner, Harold. *Who Needs God.* New York: Pocket Books, 1989.

Kurtz, Ernest, and Katherine Ketcham. *The Spirituality of Imperfection: Storytelling and the Journey to Wholeness.* New York: Bantam Books, 1992.

Merrill, Nan. *Psalms for Praying: An Invitation to Wholeness.* New York: Continuum, 1996.

Merton, Thomas. *The Way of Chuang Tzu.* Boston: Shambhala, Publications 1992.

Orsborn, Carol. *The Art of Resilience: One Hundred Paths to Wisdom and Strength in an Uncertain World.* New York: Crown, 1997.

Ram Dass. *Still Here: Embracing Aging, Changing, and Dying.* New York: Riverhead Books, 2000.

Salwak, Dale, editor. *The Wonders of Solitude.* Novato, California: New World Library, 1995.

Spenard La Russo, Carol, editor. *The Wisdom of Women.* Novato, California: New World Library, 1992.

Thompson, Marjorie J. *Soul Feast: An Invitation to the Christian Spiritual Life.* Louisville, Kentucky: Westminster John Knox Press, 1995.

Trevino, Haven. *The Tao of Healing: Meditations for Body and Spirit.* Novato, California: New World Library, 1993.

Books and Resources by Carol Orsborn

Speak the Language of Healing: Living With Breast Cancer Without Going to War. (With three co-authors.) *Berkeley, CA:* Conari Press, 1999.

The Art of Resilience: One Hundred Paths to Wisdom and Strength in an Uncertain World. New York: Crown, 1997.

Inner Excellence at Work: The Path to Meaning, Spirit and Success. Amacom Books and Peanut Press (e-book).

Return from Exile: One Woman's Journey Back to Judaism. New York: Continuum Press, 1998.

Carol Orsborn has authored ten books as well as audio workshops and books on tapes. She is also the master teacher on the interactive online retreat, My Virtual Retreat.com, based on her books and philosophy.

Web sites featuring Carol Orsborn's philosophy:

My Virtual Retreat.com
Speak Healing.com

About the Author

Carol Orsborn has written ten books applying spiritual philosophy to life challenges. Orsborn, a Phi Beta Kappa graduate of the University of California, Berkeley, earned her Masters of Theological Studies degree from Vanderbilt University, where she is currently pursuing her doctorate in religion. Her books have been published in fourteen languages and have received high honors from both the National Jewish Book Awards and the National Independent Press Association. She is currently the master teacher on the online retreat center, My Virtual Retreat.com, based on her books and philosophy. Orsborn has often been featured on the national media, sharing her wisdom on such shows as *Oprah* and *The Today Show.* She has recently relocated to Santa Monica, California, with her family.

To Our Readers

Conari Press publishes books on topics ranging from spirituality, personal growth, and relationships to women's issues, parenting, and social issues. Our mission is to publish quality books that will make a difference in people's lives—how we feel about ourselves and how we relate to one another. We value integrity, compassion, and receptivity, both in the books we publish and in the way we do business.

As a member of the community, we sponsor the Random Acts of Kindness™ Foundation, the guiding force behind Random Acts of Kindness™ Week. We donate our damaged books to nonprofit organizations, dedicate a portion of our proceeds from certain books to charitable causes, and continually look for new ways to use natural resources as wisely as possible.

Our readers are our most important resource, and we value your input, suggestions, and ideas about what you would like to see published. Please feel free to contact us, to request our latest book catalog, or to be added to our mailing list.

2550 Ninth Street, Suite 101
Berkeley, California 94710-2551
800-685-9595 • 510-649-7175
fax: 510-649-7190 • e-mail: conari@conari.com
www.conari.com